T0145177

I Believe In Destiny

MARIA LUCILIA DA SILVA

AuthorHouse™
1663 Liberty Drive
Bloomington, IN 47403
www.authorhouse.com
Phone: 833-262-8899

Because of the dynamic nature of the Internet, any web addresses or links contained in this book may have changed
since publication and may no longer be valid. The views expressed in this work are solely those of the author and do
not necessarily reflect the views of the publisher, and the publisher hereby disclaims any responsibility for them.

Any people depicted in stock imagery provided by Getty Images are models,
and such images are being used for illustrative purposes only.
Certain stock imagery © Getty Images.

This book is printed on acid-free paper.

Interior Image Credit: Amelia da Silva

ISBN: 978-1-6655-6147-1 (sc)
ISBN: 978-1-6655-6148-8 (e)

Print information available on the last page.

Published by AuthorHouse 06/03/2022

authorHOUSE

The sun was shiny and bright, dogs were barking, the creek was rushing running water to the fields on the morning of September 14, 1969. I was then a young shy 11-year-old girl, when Almirante Henrique Tenreiro made an official visit to my hometown of Figueiró da Serra, he was a prominent well-established figure in the Portuguese society at that time and his father Antonio dos Santos Tenreiro was born in Figueiró da Serra. He had been invited by the priest Jose Ventura for the inauguration of the Centro Paroquial because he had helped with the funding of that project. The ceremony entailed the unveiling of his father's bust statue, speeches, a marching band that played the national anthem revibrating a festive mood. There was a flower decorated path on the street for him to walk on as well as the other dignitaries. As far as I can remember it was a grand fabulous day, what I did not know was that day would change my destiny.

That day, Almirante Henrique Tenreiro promised to give a scholarship to a needy good student, to be decided by the primary school teacher. The teacher Mr. Profirio had two children in mind, Antonio dos Santos and me. Nobody knew how Mr. Porfirio arrived at his decision, but he picked me. There was a rumor that my mother had given a lamb to the teacher, my sister said that was not true, when I visited teacher Profirio years later he said with appreciation that my mother gave him a load of manure! Just like that my future changed forever, I was sent to live at an all-girls boarding school, Centro dos Pescadores in Costa da Caparica.

There I saw the ocean for the first time then, I could almost hear the waves from the open window of the dormitory. I was a lucky girl even dough at the time I did not feel it as I missed my family, the mountains, the fresh water, the open fields of daisies, the animals. See I was raised free in those fields almost like the sheep we owned even freer! I was expected to help with the usual farming shores, fetch water, mind the lambs, pick potatoes but there was always some time in between or at the end of the day for endless outdoor playing with friends. We played hopscotch, skipping rope, hide and seek, blindman's buff, a special ball game called pela. Because there was so little supervision there were some accidents, I fell from the veranda into a patio hitting my head on an ax playing blindman's buff. I had to be taken to the doctor in Gouveia and got six stiches, but I was lucky as it was not a deep cut or trauma. Another time I was playing at the big iron gate of Sr. Cabral's residence and broke my top front tooth when I hit my mouth against the hard iron door. There were no music or ballet classes, no TV, no organized sports nor even dolls, we played with what we had: imagination, rocks, plants, and dirt. I never felt poor on the contrary, there was plenty of love, joy, and humor! And there were the animals, we always had two dogs, sheep, lambs, goats, rams, chickens, pigs, bunnies, mare, ox. Missed the familiar faces of the towns people who all knew and cared for me, missed my grounding roots, we always walked long distances sometimes barefoot, missed the infinite blue sky during the day and the stars at night. Missed the seasons and the different fruits, I remember climbing cherry trees and eat cherries until my stomach could fit no more! I remember eating fresh sweet tangerines just stolen by my brother from my uncle's orchard during the night. Missed the killing of the pig and all the fresh dishes my mother prepared that day, special soup (sopa da matança), liver, sausages(chouriço, farrenheiras) pork tenderloins . Missed the Carnaval in February when we would dress up and take to the streets in dance and excitement burning the entrudo ao Cimo do Lugar just before Ash Wednesday. Missed the fragrance of big fields of daisies in the Spring. Missed the Rosemary bonfires and the scent of basil, the singing and dancing during São João in June with the stars above. Missed the sounds of running water and crickets in the fields. Missed the open markets with the mystery of the gypsies and the aroma of fresh cooked pork meat (febras). Specially missed my mother, family and all my friends.

Life was very structured with different activities at the boarding school, learned how to make my own bed properly, iron, embroider and other useful skills. Making the bed was useful as I would need to change it often when I peed in bed during the night, I felt very ashamed when that happened but in retrospect, I feel sorry for that young girl, I had no control with what happened when I was sleeping. We were monitored by two spinsters who lived with us for the six years I lived there. Those ladies would also make our clothing, mainly dresses. We did not wear pants then. We had two living in cooks who prepared meals for about fifty girls, the food was good and predictable we always had steak for lunch on Sundays. On Sundays we would also go to the church which was just across the street. That first Fall I attended Middle School via remote learning. There was a teacher in the room, and we would learn different subjects taught via the television. I was always very engaged and eager to learn as I wanted to show everyone, I was a good student.

During school vacations like Christmas, Easter and Summer I would get rides back to my hometown from my Tio Leonardo. As I got older, I would catch a bus to Caçilhas, a ferry boat to Terreiro do Paço and walk to Santa Aplónia to catch a train. I always marveled at the sites from Lisbon to the Gouveia station and felt so sophisticated and confident. When I arrived in Figueiró I felt incredibly special, happy, and loved. Before leaving from Costa da Caparica during the Summertime I would go to the beach in the morning and afternoon with lunch and siesta in between. Those were the best times, I loved bathing in the ocean and learned to swim with my friends. At night after dinner, we would also go for a walk near the ocean through Rua dos Pescadores where we would buy ice cream. Rua dos Pescadores was always packed with happy people. We would go back home licking our ice cream, joking, and smelling the gardenias spilling over to the streets from the beautiful beach cottages. I loved showing off my tan when I got to Figueiró, most of those people never saw the ocean, they lived their whole lives rooted in the Serra da Estrela's hills tending to the animals and their farms. That could have been my future as well, I was groomed by my brother and sisters to do many farm things, tend the sheep flock, feed the chickens and pigs, weed and water the crops, dig potatoes, pick corn and beans, harvest wheat, milk the sheep and goats. I was directed to do certain tasks on my own. One time I was told to bring lunch to the shepherd, I carried it in a basket that sat on top of my head for about five miles. Because I was barefoot, I tripped my toes on a stone and dropped the basket with the food on the dirt road. I salvaged what I could, pored some water in the soup, Caldo Verde pot to make up for what was lost and gave it to Chico when I got to the Quinta do Veneno. He was not fooled by my resourcefulness, right after his first taste he got so mad that he threw all his lunch down the hill. I was somewhat concerned but left him there fuming and went back home. I also helped with the harvesting of the grapes and making the wine by stepping on the grapes. I could drink the sweet wine Jurpiga when I was little, I loved it. I saw my mother make cheese every day, so I learned from watching her. I rode on top of the mares on my own, we had different ones through the years. We had a very wild white with black dots mare who if she felt like it would trough me on top of prickly wild blackberry bushes. I remember one time when as I arrived in town the mare got very startled with some noise and took off so fast on that cobblestone street making me fear for my life. Someone must have come to my aid and made her stop. At the end of the Summer, I was always sent off with the Santa Eufémia feast which was celebrated on September sixteen every year. The arrayal was on the fifteen, my father would kill a goat for stew and roasting, my mother would make biscuits and sweet rice. At night after the goat stew dinner and the procession there would be an outdoor dance listening to a local band music ending with beautiful fireworks and gatherings by the Capela of Santa Eufemia. I remember it was a night of romance and I always felt beautiful, I mainly danced with other girls but was hoping the young man would have their eyes on me. This was an event that brought a lot of people to the town, my Tio Leonardo would visit with his family. They would often have lunch with us on the sixteen which consisted of chicken soup (canja), roasted goat with potatoes, melon, grapes, figs, sweet rice, and biscuits. The next day I would catch a ride back to Lisbon with, Tio Leonardo. The road between Figueiró and Coimbra was so winding that it would often make me very nauseous, there was this time that I threw up making me feel so bad for the inconvenience and stinky mess.

When I finished the Middle School, I started attending the High School at the Liçeu National the Almada to complete my secondary education. I would take a bus from Costa da Caparica to Almada via Capuchos and attend the different classes during the day. The girls would have classes in the morning and the boys would have them in the afternoon, we would exchange notes by leaving pieces of papers on the desks. I used to hang out with the same group of girls, Isabel, Zé, Luisa, Manela, Lurdes. I had more freedom during High School, we would sometimes catch a ferry boat to Terreiro do Paço and go to the movies. I took a lot of those trips to the downtown of Lisbon with Isabel, we would do a lot of walking and window shopping. Those streets were always packed with people, that was where people would buy shoes, clothes and all the fashion accessories, there were no malls back then. We would buy roasted chestnuts as we could not resist them, we would stop at Pastelaria Suiça for an expresso coffee and a sweet treat. The coffee aroma and the sight of the lined-up pastries was enough to make our senses happy. As time went by, I spent more and more time with Isabel, she would invite me to spend weekends and even some vacations with her family. Her mom was an incredibly good cook, she subscribed to French magazines and would often try those recipes. I had Fondue for the first time ever at Isabel's house, dona Maria das Dores was a woman with opinions and strong convictions, she was knowledgeable and generous. During an Easter vacation they took me to Algarve and stayed at their monte not far from Lagos. It was hot and we sunbathed at the Praia da Rocha. On Easter's day Isabel's father roasted a whole goat in an outdoors wooded oven which was so delicious. That vacation was very enjoyable. It was like the Caiano family had adopted me, Isabel had no other siblings, and I was like a sister to her. I was a submissive sister and went along with everything she was doing, we camped in Fonte da Telha one time, and I remember getting sun burned. Isabel's skin was more tolerant to the sun than mine.

Fascismo was the controlling regime in Portugal during those years, Marcello Caetano followed Salazar's footsteps, both were authoritarian leaders incorporating social Catholicism. Portugal was at war in the African Colonies, Angola, Mozambique and Guiné. There had been growing discontent and some opposition, the PIDE police persecuted all the opponents of the regime. Several military officers who opposed the war formed the MFA to overthrow the government in a military coup. The coup had two secret signals, the first was the song "E Depois do Adeus" by Paulo de Carvalho which aired at 10:55pm on April 24th. The second signal came at 12:20am on April 25th when Radio Renascença broadcasted the song "Grandola Vila Morena". The MFA gave the signals to take over strategic points of power in the country. In April 25Th 1974 there were no shots or casualties but later the Caetano government resigned. Despite repeated appeals from the Captains of April advising civilians to stay home, thousands of Portuguese took the streets supporting the military. Some of the insurgents placed carnations in the gun barrels, this involvement turned the military coup into a popular revolution using the language of socialism and democracy. Caetano fled to Brazil as well as many of their supporters. Almirante Henrique Tenreiro who was the Centro dos Pescadores Patron also fled to Brazil. The Antonio dos Santos Tenreiro's bust statue was thrown in a well in Figueiró da Serra. This statue was later found and placed back but no one found out who had done this destructive act.

There were no classes and some of the students went to Lisbon and participated in the demonstrations I however did not. That day again impacted my future, shortly after that day the Centro dos Pescadores was closed. Fortunately, Isabel's parents opened their doors of their home in Monte da Caparica to me and I was able to finish the Liçeu. I am forever grateful to them as I was with them for over a year and did not pay room and board. The Caiano family were very curious to see my hometown and we all went there, they somehow slept at our house, we only had two bedrooms. In the morning I remember hearing loud noises coming from the bathroom as Isabel's father was taking a cold shower. We did not have hot water! They loved Figueiró and were glad to meet my family. My mother gave them a few cheeses she had made; Isabel loved my mother. My mother Maria dos Anjos Pires Moreira was full of enthusiasm for life. She was ambitious, determined, she was kind and she loved to feed everyone, and you would often hear her laugh. She made the best cheese, and she would negotiate the best prices for it in the open markets. My father Joaquim dos Santos was a good man but he was more reserved. He served his family, he used to plow the fields with his oxes for money, but he would do his parents farm for free. He also served his country; he was in the Portuguese army during World War II and was stationed in the Açores Island. He loved to drink and hang out at the tavern with other men. Sometimes he drank too much, and he would come home wanting to beat my mother. All the kids, my two sisters, brother and I, would surround my mother to protect her, she was also quick on her feet, and she would hide, she never got any bruises.

Meanwhile in school everything had changed too, there were a lot of meetings led by some students. One of those leaders was Telmo da Silva, he was so charming, tall, and good looking. I was in the audience just trying to pay attention to what they were saying but at the same time I was fantasizing about a romantic involvement with Telmo. I knew of him because I saw him upfront on the stage, but he did not have any idea who I was. He was always talking with passion and conviction about the fundamental freedoms and rights of all human beings. All human beings should have access to what they aspired and nourished to equal opportunities and growth. Socialism doctrines would be invoked followed by open discussions in those meetings at Liçeu. I liked those principals of equality specially since I always felt inferior, somehow deficient in the polished ways of the city life, but I was never that passionate or stirred to action by those ideas. Still, I was pulled to attend those large general meetings at the Gym mainly to see Telmo.

Telmo was borne in Angola while his father worked for the development of the railroads. A lot of the Portuguese families of that era took advantage of the opportunities offered in the country's colonies. Telmo said he played with snakes when he was just a toddler in the tropical sun of the African continent. He was only two years old when his family traveled by boat back to Portugal, had they stayed maybe they would not have survived the war that came later. Had he stayed maybe we would not have ever met.

It was the end of the seventh grade, I had finished with good grades of course, proud of being the first in my family to finish High School. A group of friends decided to organize an end of the year picnic. It was a large group; my close friends all went as well as others including Telmo. We did a lot of walking to get to Fonte da Telha but was all worth it, the weather was great, the sun was bright and shining, we played a lot of games, we talked, we ate, we took pictures. We were an optimistic group, proud of what we had accomplished, and the feeling was of celebration and possibility. Would it be possible that Telmo would like me? I know there were many other girls my age who liked him too, who would not? He was just a gorgeous attractive young man with a warm smile who might have heard my heart's longing. We got to talk that day and we set up a date at the Costa da Caparica beach. That day I was high with love and anticipation, my heart and soul wanted him, and the vibe was reciprocal, the sand, the ocean, and the sea breeze also helped the expansion of mutual feelings of two young people in love.

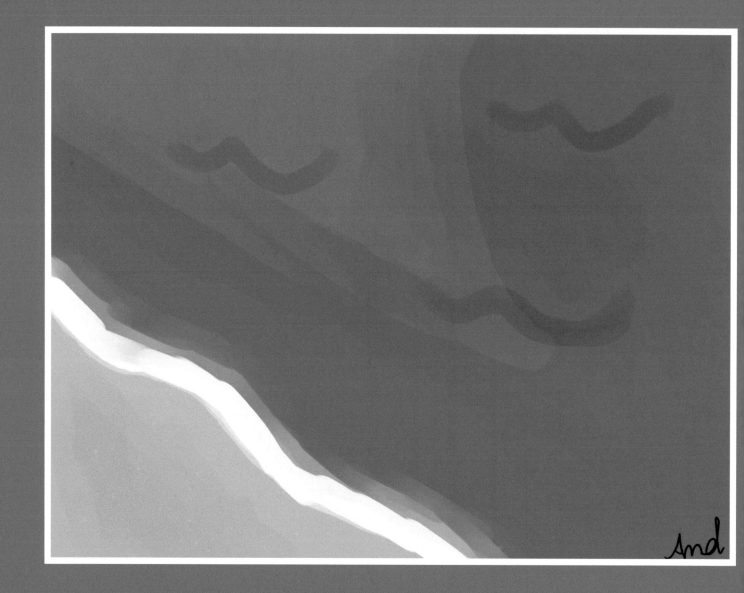

I left for the Summer to be with my family in Figueiró, Telmo and I would correspond romantic letters where we continued to express our love for one another. My older sister had immigrated to the United States of America to be with her husband, she became a USA citizen and had the opportunity to sponsor the rest of the family to be with her. That Summer my family decided to sell all the farm animals, made all necessary arrangements, and obtained the permanent resident visa permits to travel to América, the land of golden opportunities. My father, mother, sister Gloria, brother-in-law, little niece Christina and I left Portugal in October 1976 in search of a brighter future in America.

In October 1977 Telmo followed me across the Atlantic Ocean, we got married at the Pawtucket City Hall that same year in December. It was a very casual ceremony just the godparents of marriage, the Caetanos and my immediate family, parents, sister Candida and Gloria. My parents and my family were disappointed as it was not a church wedding, but they went along with our plans. We had no money or monetary help from anyone, we started with nothing. There was no honeymoon. All the pieces of furniture we had were bought at Salvation Army. None of that mattered as we were young and innocent and finally together.

The dreaming days were over, I was going to Rhode Island College, but I was not doing very well in school. I felt overwhelmed and out of place most of the time. Sometimes I took some rides to school with my friend Madalena in her small Volkswagen Beetle. Eventually I got a second shift job at Hasbro assembling plastic toys, got paid by the amount assembled. I learned to drive, took the driver's license, and bought my first car, a green Hornet without power steering. As I was driving to attend classes one morning, I got into a car accident, I took too long to turn and bumped into another car. I used up most of Telmo's money for the repairs and he would never let me forget it. On the morning of February 6, 1978, I drove myself to Rhode Island College, but the classes were canceled due to a snowstorm. I was lucky as I made it safely home, but many people got stuck in the snow and had to abandon their cars on the streets and highways, it was the infamous 1978 blizzard. It took more than a week to clean and clear all the roads, there was no work or school. We walked everywhere; the government gave us some money for food. It was Telmo's first Winter in the United States and my second, our bodies were still not acclimatized, and we did not have proper coats. Life was not easy, but we were young and hopeful, we learned how to survive from the other local Portuguese immigrants. We could always count on the support of my older sister Candida and her husband Américo, we had many meals at their kitchen table. I will always be grateful for their generosity and hospitality.

I believe in Destiny; how else would you explain our union? Telmo was born in the tropical Angola, and I was born in the small town of Beira Alta, our lives crossed in Almada and made it all the way to América. You may say that you make your own destiny, but it was not me that made the decision to leave Figueiró da Serra to go study in Costa da Caparica, it was done for me, and I am incredibly grateful for the adventure and for the journey. There were no gold opportunities for me, never made it to be rich and famous, did not even finish college but I always worked, and we made a good life, not perfect but good. Most of all our marriage allowed us to have two wonderful children Marco and Marta, their lives are more enriched because we came to América, the land of opportunities.

Printed in the United States
by Baker & Taylor Publisher Services